ANATOMY OF A
LEADER

Responsibility

Vision

Personal Touch

Heart

Fortitude

Flexibility

Self Motivation

D0559049

CARL MAYS

Illustrations by Tom Barg

TABLE OF CONTENTS

THE HEART OF A LEADER

Having the heart of a leader means developing an appreciation for who you are and recognizing your own strengths and qualifications. You can then concentrate on acquiring additional skills that contribute to the achievement of your goals. Many people often compare themselves to others without realizing the value of their own potential. They envy careers or successes that appear to be more attractive than their own. This negative comparison is damaging. Don't do it. Instead, concentrate on being the best You possible.

You are somebody, an important person and a unique individual with great abilities and versatility. Unfortunately, many people don't realize what they have and never come close to taking full advantage of their gifts and resources. The real challenge, and the real reward, is to take who you are and what you are capable of doing, and create the means to achieve your dreams. Having the heart of a leader is to discover self-reliance, to acquire the stamina to persevere, and to develop the vital qualities necessary for success.

3

PRACTICE SELF-AWARENESS

Self-awareness is a powerful human resource. It means having a valid opinion of yourself and being aware of all your positive qualities without arrogance or conceit. A good self-image contributes to the successful attainment of your goals and determines the way you live your life. With an authentic opinion of yourself you are able to evaluate your talents in a sincere, uncritical manner.

People often have a tendency to minimize their potential, and unfavorably compare their own unique individuality to others. They have incorrect images of themselves and accept these distortions as truths. An honest opinion of yourself will never permit an attitude of negative personal worth. If you wish to become successful, it is important to understand your importance. The heart of a leader is a trademark of the self-aware person.

REMAIN CONFIDENT

Successful people still encounter disappointments and frustrations, but it is the way they respond to problems that makes them different from those who are overwhelmed by difficult situations. The challenge is to remain optimistic and confident. Being enthusiastic about what you can accomplish and the means by which you will realize your dreams is what confidence is all about.

Problems can cause unhappiness and defeat you if you allow them to. Don't try to avoid the reality of possible delays or complications. Instead, remain confident; the ultimate attainment of your goals is within reach. Take advantage of the powerful resources that are already within you. At the heart of confidence is determination, self-reliance and a security in your own purpose.

EXPECT SUCCESS

Expectations make all the difference in your quest for success. They can be more important than aspirations or desires. You must expect to succeed. Remain optimistic about the outcome of your goals, despite temporary disappointments. Concentrate on your preparation instead of assuming that you have a negligible chance for success.

The famous story of Babe Ruth is a good example of the power of expectation. After hitting a home run into the section of the stands he pointed to, he told reporters that it had never entered his mind that he would not fulfill his promise. He had his heart-set on hitting a home run and nothing was going to prevent him from accomplishing his goal. It is truly amazing how capable people are of living up to their own expectations.

Everyone has had, at one time or another, experiences which were painful or unpleasant. Some individuals are destroyed by them, while others are able to not only survive intact, but discover the "backbone" to allow them to become successful.

Scott Coleman's life changed forever when he was suddenly paralyzed from the neck down in an accident. It took him two years to regain the use of his biceps. Later, through hard work and rehabilitation, he was able to establish a successful career as an account executive. He proved he was equal to the challenge in such creative ways as dialing the telephone with his tongue. Scott gives much of the credit for his success to the people who support him. But it was his courage that enabled him to turn what could have been a disaster into the adventure he made it.

Courage is manifested in many different ways, not only by those people who have suffered physical traumas. It is also apparent in individuals who choose a goal and exhibit the determination, self-reliance, and energy needed to realize their ambition.

PERSEVERE

To be determined is to confront adversity with
confidence and persistence, without ever considering
the possibility of failure. Certain individuals are
able to overcome seemingly insurmountable odds
rather than yielding to them. They become role
models for anyone who has the motivation and need
to achieve exceptional goals.

Beethoven triumphed over deafness to compose
majestic music. Milton defeated blindness to write
words of depth and beauty. Helen Keller, who
could neither see, hear, nor speak, achieved more
than most people can imagine. Although Louisa
Mae Alcott was told by an editor that she had no
writing ability and should forget writing as a career,
she produced Little Women, as well as other
famous novels. When Walt Disney submitted his
first drawings for publication, he was told he had
no talent. These people, and many others like them,
define the essence of courage, strength, determination, and perseverance.

KNOW YOURSELF

It is important to believe in what you are doing and to know who you are. In order to become a leader, you must be realistic about yourself. Consider what strengths you possess, and what you are capable of achieving. If you have confidence in your abilities and make wise use of your personal resources, you will be successful.

People often overlook their very best qualities. Unfortunately they don't realize how unique they are or how unlimited their potential. They remain unaware of their capabilities, and deny the possibility that they, too, can aspire to goals previously beyond their reach. They remain steadfast in their belief that they are incapable of success. Don't make the mistake of thinking attributes such as enthusiasm, patience, perseverance, and adaptability are minor details of little or no use to real success. Individuals with these valuable attitudes are being sought in every field.

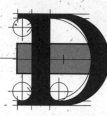EVELOP GOOD HABITS

Everyone makes mistakes, but good habits can prevent many of them. People with poor habits often defeat themselves. Most competitions are determined by errors made by the losers. A successful person forms habits that are consistent with the type of individual he or she aspires to become. Take full advantage of your beneficial habits and eliminate those that are negative or unprofitable because they determine physical, mental, and emotional attitudes. Keep those that are consistent with a person who attains worthwhile goals.

It takes strength and determination to develop good habits. It takes fortitude to maintain newly acquired behaviors and not return to previous ones, but you can do it. Good habits are surprisingly important if you wish to succeed.

Physical fitness is an essential element for a leader. Your energy levels will be significantly enhanced if you maintain a healthy body. The more you increase your strength and energy, the more you will accomplish. The growth in your stamina leads to a continuing routine of invigorating exercise.

Daily physical activity not only promotes a strong, healthy body, but increases vitality, and stimulates ambition. Resolve to do some type of exercise regularly. Rigorous or extensive conditioning is not required – just ten minutes of calisthenics and thirty minutes of walking can be immensely beneficial. Also, consider a wholesome and nutritious diet as essential. It's not always easy to maintain the discipline of a fitness program, but life is much more enjoyable when you're energetic and in good physical condition.

HEALTH AND SUCCESS

As part of a program for success, the importance of caring for and preserving your health cannot be overstated. More major corporations are installing exercise facilities and offering special meals for employees. They also provide time and space for a regular fitness program. Hotels have discovered the value of providing exercise equipment for their customers. Nutritious meals are now listed on most hotel and restaurant menus.

Athletes have always known, and now the business world is beginning to understand just how beneficial exercise and healthy bodies are for success. It's not always easy to eat sensibly or to participate in a regular schedule of physical activity, but the results are immeasurable.

PLAN AHEAD

Just as you strengthen your body with vigorous exercise, you need to dedicate as much energy toward the attainment of your ultimate goal. As you consider the direction of your ambition, it is important to visualize smaller, more attainable increments, the steps needed to gain desired results. Just as it is virtually impossible for athletes to deliver a peak performance without the proper conditioning and preparation, it is, at best, extremely difficult to achieve any goal without meticulous planning.

Many people have a very distorted notion of how things are actually accomplished. In sports, for example, they only see athletes suddenly becoming champions; they are unaware of the effort that preceded the triumphs. They watched Jackie Joyner-Kersee and Michael Johnson win Olympic Gold, not knowing the countless hours they worked to attain world-class recognition. In business, individuals might notice a company that is successful and decide they are able to duplicate, or even surpass, such enterprises without realizing all the initial effort that was needed. Their downfall occurs because of the lack of planning and preparation.

SET SPECIFIC GOALS

A specific goal makes it easier to understand what you want to achieve. Your plan should be stated in a way that leaves no question as to the final outcome. When you design a plan with a definite objective, it puts you in charge of the final result. Being precise will give your ideas more clarity and direction; they will have greater purpose and meaning. It also helps you work harder to succeed.

Many famous athletes and important business leaders have experienced rejections. Irving Stone was turned away 16 times before his book, Lust For Life, was published. Ron Guidry almost quit baseball when he was sent down to the minors. Mary Kay Ash sold a total of $1.50 at her first beauty show. What these three successful people have in common is that they did not surrender, nor did they abandon their specific, achievable goals. Within each was the strong desire to succeed and an unwillingness to settle for something less than their dreams.

PUT GOALS IN WRITING

When goals are written they become more concrete. In addition, writing down your intentions will help you to remember them. The physical act of putting on paper various concepts, strategies, and guidelines reinforces them in your mind. You then, become more aware of what is necessary to achieve these goals. After you have written your objectives, be sure to review them as often as possible. Although revisions can be made if circumstances change, it is necessary to create as decisive a plan as possible.

Committing to paper exactly what is desired and how to achieve it is a technique that produces positive results. Business leaders can develop programs to enhance their rate of success and athletes could describe how they will improve their game or devise strategies specific to their next opponent. What you write down, what you truly believe in, and what your mind accepts will determine what you achieve.

REACH AND ACHIEVE

There are a variety of plans out there for attaining goals but, ultimately, the depth of your commitment decides whether or not they will be achieved. Simply wishing success will somehow happen cannot cause or even influence the achievement of your objectives.

Optimism, enthusiasm, intensity, and excitement are the basis of motivation and success. However, much is dependent on how wisely you channel those qualities. To become reality, intentions must be accompanied by a measure of energy and effort. Reach out and grab with both hands what you want. You are then in charge of your own life and have a specific purpose. Develop the determination to achieve your plans regardless of obstacles, criticism, or situations. Don't settle for less than the complete fulfillment of your dreams.

LEND A HELPING HAND

A successful endeavor can begin with something as simple as a handshake. Potential customers or clients who are greeted warmly, are often satisfied that they were right to do business with your organization. It is just as important to lend a helping hand to those who may need it. No one can succeed alone. Even athletes in individual sports, such as tennis or gymnastics, credit parents, friends, and coaches with helping them along the way.

Offer your support to people striving to achieve a specific purpose. You may one day receive the benefit of their assistance and expertise. A "Peanuts" cartoon by Charles Shultz showed Linus admiring his hands. He becomes excited about the potential they hold, he thinks that with them he could become a great leader, a professional athlete, a surgeon, a renowned author, or even the President of the United States. Think of the possibilities if everyone looked at his or her hands this way.

17

SEEK SOLUTIONS

Everyone experiences problems or difficulties on occasion. Most people don't realize that what they view as frustrating interruptions, delays, or complications can actually be beneficial. They can help you become more determined. Leaders must have a belief in themselves that is more powerful than the problems, inconveniences, or obstructions they encounter.

It is also important to define a situation before you take action. Simply defining the problem will help you see the opportunity within and create an even better solution. By working hand in hand with other team members you can often discover outstanding possibilities that lead to new plans and ideas.

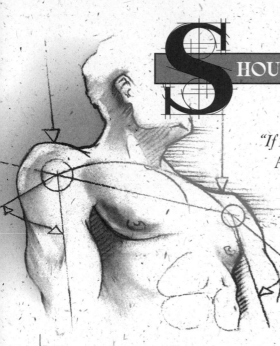

SHOULDER RESPONSIBILITY

"If it is to be, it is up to me." Although problems may arise which discourage ambitions, a leader does not sit on the sidelines and hope that someone else will assume authority or resolve the situation. When a major decision must be made, the outstanding individual does not try to pass the buck.

Shouldering responsibility is an essential characteristic of a successful leader. The motto of Winston Churchill, one of the 20th century's leading statesmen, was: "The price of greatness is responsibility." Conscientious, reliable people, who can excel under pressure, meet obligations, and assume leadership, are increasingly being sought by the business world, and virtually every organization in society. People are motivated by a fair, but decisive, leader who is in command of the situation. If you build a reputation as someone willing to make important decisions and to "shoulder responsibility," you have an excellent chance to succeed in any endeavor.

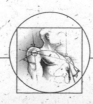

 SHOULDER TO SHOULDER

Each individual in an organization must make a choice as to what role he or she will play. The choice is either to actively participate or simply go through the motions from the sidelines. Being a reliable member of an organization means contributing to the success of everyone. It is important for each person to believe that what he or she provides to the group is valuable. Realizing that success increases when everyone works toward a common goal is a powerful incentive for cooperation. Together, individuals have a combined strength that is unbeatable. A united group is almost assured of success.

It is amazing what can happen when colleagues are committed to a task and committed to one another. Working shoulder to shoulder with associates builds loyalty, commitment, and enthusiasm. In the 1980 Olympics, the U.S. hockey team was ranked seventh in a field of eight teams. Working together, they won game after game, and gained enormous confidence with each win. In the final game, it was the undefeated American team against Russia, the expected gold medal winner. That game became one of the greatest upsets in the history of sports when the U.S. team won 4 - 3. There were twenty young men on the American team. As individuals, they were good; as a team they were the best in the world.

ATTEND TO DETAILS

People do not build successful businesses or develop into champion caliber athletes in a matter of weeks. Nor do they become "overnight successes." Significant achievements are made up of small, steady actions. It is both beneficial and logical to complete one step at a time in order to achieve your ultimate goal. Methodically schedule and organize your objectives. Be sure that you are actually doing what is essential, and in the appropriate order, no matter how insignificant the process may seem at the time.

If you adhere to the progressive development of your plan, success will be the ultimate result. When you prepare for even the smallest of detail, fewer unexpected inconveniences will affect the outcome of your ambitions. Planning makes all the difference in the world.

INITIATE AND ACCOMPLISH

An ancient Greek proverb states: "The beginning is half of your action." Many ventures are not successful simply because they are never begun. Initiating an endeavor is usually the most difficult part. The realization of your goal is possible, however, if you are unafraid of the responsibilities required for success. An important point to remember: Do not procrastinate. By the time you finally do begin, it may be too late.

Many times it would be easier to postpone a decision, to lower your standards, or to simply quit trying. But, with determination comes an understanding of what it means to be a successful leader. If you are resolute, and want to realize your potential, you will eagerly assume all efforts necessary to succeed. A tremendous sense of accomplishment will make all the hard work worthwhile.

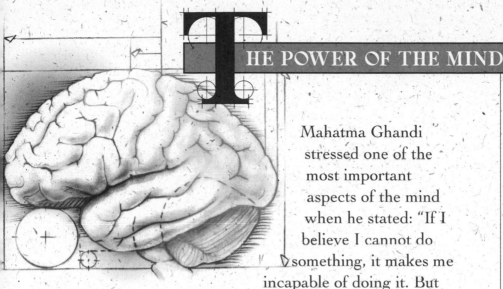

THE POWER OF THE MIND

Mahatma Ghandi stressed one of the most important aspects of the mind when he stated: "If I believe I cannot do something, it makes me incapable of doing it. But when I believe I can, I acquire the ability to do it, even if I did not have the ability in the beginning."

Think about it. You have within you the resources to accomplish even those goals which may have been dismissed as unobtainable. Research conducted on the power of the subconscious indicates that physical changes do occur when the body is influenced by the brain. There is no doubt the mind and the body are interrelated, that an individual's state of mind determines physical abilities. This remarkable combination can be released through a positive attitude, which leads to success in sports, in business, and in all areas of life. Henry Ford put it another way when he said: "If you decide you can or can't do something – you are right."

THINK LIKE A LEADER

All too frequently individuals choose not to believe they can become leaders. Because of the misguided notion that leadership is beyond their qualifications or talents, they make it impossible to realize their dreams. In the history of humankind, there has been only one you. Never again will there be anyone else with your exact combination of talent, imagination, and potential. If you do not develop these special and unique qualities, the world will be denied the experience of your distinct abilities.

The mind, which has limitless creativity, is the world's most powerful tool. Let it work for you, allow it to give you the confidence required to become a leader. If you think like a leader, you will become a leader.

TAP INTO YOUR SUBCONSCIOUS

Imagine you have a problem that appears to have no logical solution. What type of approach can you use to find a satisfactory result? One way is to allow your subconscious to work for you. Begin to think positively and constructively about the situation. Do not be tempted to settle for makeshift or unsatisfactory alternatives simply because they appear to be quick and easy.

The subconscious mind stores every single thing you see, hear, read, or experience, and is amazingly effective at making use of this accumulated knowledge. An idea may suddenly emerge, seemingly out of nowhere. However, nothing simply occurs at random. Rather, these thoughts are your mind at work. Make use of this powerful resource, and you just might be surprised by the results.

BE CREATIVE

True creativity is doing a common thing uncommonly well. It is possible, through inventiveness, to bring something into existence that has never been created before. Essentially, however, authentic creativity involves regarding an existing idea, object, or method with a different perspective. Nobel Prize winning physician Albert Szent-Gyorgyi explained this concept by stating: "Discovery consists of looking at the same thing as everyone else and thinking something different."

Each person is born with creative potential, but many individuals create barriers to their ingenuity because they fear ridicule or failure. So, in order to prevent embarrassment and discomfort, they conform; they become like everyone else. Do not allow temporary distress to suffocate your innate cleverness. The rewards will transcend any problems encountered along the way. The human mind is an enormous creative force – benefit by using it.

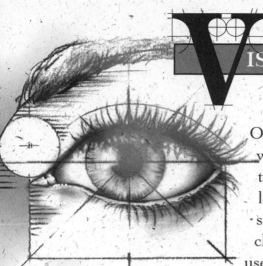

VISUALIZE RESULTS

One important way in which you can develop the qualities required for leadership, as well as significantly improve your chances for success, is to use the principle of visualization. Visualization is forming vivid pictures in your mind. It is also seeing things happen before they actually do. Through visualization, your imagination can show you what you want to accomplish. Once these creative thoughts are established, you can then transform them into reality.

The idea of seeing pictures in your mind may seem to be an unusual way to help yourself achieve success, but in reality you have been doing it your entire life. The concept of visualization is no different than children using their imaginations. It is merely an adult version of make-believe. However, this time, the daydream can become a reality.

# VIEW FROM THE MIND'S EYE

Leadership is particularly effective when it includes the use of creative visualization. As you determine exactly what you want to visualize, be certain of your ultimate intent. If you have sufficient interest and imagination, you will be capable of seeing your ambition clearly. It is important to visualize all the possible results before you decide upon a course of action. Imagine the results you want in order to make the chosen outcome a reality. Specifically visualizing a goal in this way, enables you to obtain it. This activity is especially powerful when combined with the belief in your ability to achieve success. Things do not simply happen. You make them happen, and visualization plays a large part in each accomplishment.

Leaders expect to become successful, resolve difficulties, find solutions, create opportunities, and attain goals. They utilize every resource, including visualization, to do what is required to achieve corporate and personal objectives.

KEEP OBJECTIVES IN SIGHT

Florence Chadwick wanted to be the first woman ever to swim the English Channel. For years she trained and disciplined herself to keep going long after her body needed rest. When the big day arrived, she set out to realize her dream. Things went well until she neared the coast of England, where a heavy fog and cold, rough waters impeded her progress. Not realizing she was within a few hundred yards of the shore, Florence Chadwick became completely exhausted and could no longer swim. She was heartbroken to learn how close she had been to reaching the coast. She told news reporters: "I'm not offering excuses, but I think I could have made it if I had been able to see my goal."

Later she tried again and, this time, she developed a mental image of the English coastline. She memorized every feature of the distant landscape and held it clearly in her mind. Once again she was hindered by fog and a frigid, turbulent sea, but this time she was able to accomplish what she had set out to do because she never lost sight of her objective. The expertise to envision possibilities, the power to remain focused, and the ability to visualize, all contribute to the acquisition of goals. Amazing things can and do happen when we keep our objectives in sight.

29

BE ENTHUSIASTIC

There is nothing quite like enthusiasm, no matter what you are doing. It creates a sense of anticipation, optimism, and even fun. Visualization inspired by such enthusiasm becomes very powerful. You become genuinely involved with each idea. One of the greatest qualities of a leader is the dynamic interest to pursue a goal or an objective. This enthusiasm is impressive, as well as contagious, and can create momentum.

To use visualization deliberately and effectively, it is imperative that you create a clear idea or picture of what you desire and then focus on it often and in a variety of ways. Thinking about it makes it real. Successful people usually find what they are looking for because they expect to find it. Enthusiastic people can actually see themselves holding the trophy, hearing the cheering crowd and smelling the roses in the winner's circle.

In order to become successful, the members of sports teams or business organizations, must work together. The best efforts of all members compliment each other. An especially important aspect of group activity is listening. By being attentive, you can benefit from important information, gain new perspectives, and receive encouragement.

Listening presents an opportunity to appreciate the knowledge, visions, and creativity of other people. It is a skill that is often overlooked, although it contributes to efficient communication. To listen enables you to learn from the advice of more experienced associates. It also teaches you to be considerate of the viewpoints of others, even if you do not agree with what you hear. Sometimes people are so preoccupied with their own problems and projects they forget to enjoy, appreciate, or listen to others. Take the time to listen. You will be well rewarded.

EXPRESS GRATITUDE

A positive approach to your work and life is to appreciate hearing the thoughts, ideas, and observations of others. Everyone needs help to accomplish goals. Be thankful for the people who give you their attention, advice, and support. They will inspire you to develop your potential. You may not always be in agreement with them, but you should feel fortunate to know that associates or team members will tell you what you need to hear. Finally, thank those who have assisted you in any way. It gives you the opportunity to tell them how much their efforts have been, and continue to be, appreciated.

LISTEN TO YOUR CONSCIENCE

The media is permeated with stories concerning the unethical behavior of prominent members of society. Athletes are fined for unsportsmanlike conduct and the misuse of drugs, while business people and politicians are involved in scandals concerning fraud, dishonesty, and corrupt corporate practices. There has never been a greater need for professional ethics and honorable, respectable leaders.

Your conscience should be the standard by which choices are made. These decisions are revealed in your daily activities and relationships. Leaders need to be stable and reliable, refusing to be influenced by circumstances or unethical acquaintances. Listen to the guidance of your conscience, even though there will be situations where adherence to your own high personal standards will be difficult. You are the only one who can decide your course of action. Have the courage to live up to your own convictions. This will enable you to make the correct decisions and to enhance your chance for success.

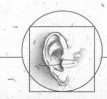

CHOOSE ASSOCIATES WISELY

Be wise when you choose your associates. You are fortunate if you know positive people who share the same high personal and moral standards and ambitions. These goal-oriented individuals are willing to take the risks necessary to succeed. They will challenge you to turn what might have been considered a disaster into an adventure. From them you will receive support. Such dynamic individuals are a rich source of knowledge and inspiration. They refrain from being negative or critical because they understand the effects of ungracious comments about personal interests or goals.

On the average, people hear seven criticisms to every one compliment. Most remember the negative remarks far longer than the positive statements. Those associates or friends who are in agreement with your desire for success won't criticize or think you are reckless or foolish. Hearing positive comments can reinforce your worth and can promote a stronger willingness to work for success.

COMPLIMENT OTHERS

Much is revealed about the character of a person by how he or she gives and receives compliments. Those who react to sincere praise negatively reveal an unfortunate lack of self-esteem. The most sincere way to respond to a compliment is to graciously accept it. Making complimentary statements shows self-confidence; being able to express genuine respect and admiration for another is exhibiting one of the significant qualities of leadership.

Choose what you consider to be the best attribute of your associates and praise them for it. Specifically mention their positive points. This can cause an increase in their confidence and self-respect, and they certainly will appreciate your regard. Bestowing compliments is an excellent indication of consideration. You should look for reasons to compliment others. You will not only enhance their morale and refresh their disposition, but you most likely will receive more courtesy and respect in return.

35

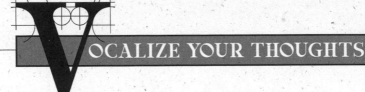

VOCALIZE YOUR THOUGHTS

Have you ever had an idea you wanted to share at a meeting, but hesitated because it was your opinion and you believed no one would be interested? All too often someone else introduces a similar notion which is readily accepted, and you're left with feelings of frustration because you didn't speak out.

A leader doesn't wait for someone else to determine the course of action and outcome of plans. Nor does that person wait until a colleague or associate indicates agreement with suggestions before responding. Always provide positive reinforcement, and never be critical. Let people know you are grateful for their help and your opportunities. The more you take the initiative by speaking your mind, the more influence and control you will have in your life.

COMMUNICATE EFFECTIVELY

The ability to communicate in a courteous, appropriate, and tactful manner is an extremely important quality all leaders must demonstrate. The way you speak is a reflection of your personality and intelligence. It represents both yourself and your organization. When introductions are being made, a confident person is often the first to initiate them, and is courteous with all contacts. Politeness is contagious; be the one to create an epidemic.

Through phone conversations and personal contacts, your verbal abilities make an impression on associates, co-workers, team members, and customers. Talking with others who have had similar experiences or are in the same profession enables you to learn from their successes and mistakes. Receiving and communicating information clearly and cordially is extremely important in the attainment of your goals.

ASK WHAT IF?

Many people are afraid of being different. They believe that they must conform to what others have deemed as appropriate. But you don't have to be satisfied with mediocrity. Allow yourself, instead, to explore the imaginative, even revolutionary, ideas your mind invents. Being creative does mean taking risks, but anything worth doing involves a measure of uncertainty and chance.

Do not yield to the fear of failure. Instead, keep in mind the potential for success. It is also important to share your innovative and unique concepts with others. Permit them to join in the fun of exploring unique possibilities. In addition, vocalizing your ideas tends to make them more real.

Reflect upon your childhood daydreams and games of make-believe. You can use these same techniques today. And, your current dreams can actually come true, especially if you ask yourself this important question: *"What if?"* What if it were tried this way instead of that way? What if the team used a new offense? What if I actually did ask for a raise? What if the company tried a new marketing strategy? *"What if…?"*

RUN A STRONG RACE

She was a premature baby and weighed only four and one-half pounds. At four years of age, she had double pneumonia and scarlet fever, leaving her with a paralyzed left leg. But, with the positive influence of her mother, she had the courage and determination to initiate a plan for success. In her ninth year, she did away with her brace and took her first unaided steps. In high school, she entered a race and finished last, but she didn't quit. With much effort she began to win races in college and, finally, in the Olympics. Racing against the greatest female runners of the time, Wilma Rudolph won three gold medals.

If a child from a poor family, who was never expected to walk or even live, not to mention, run, can achieve such outstanding results, imagine what you can accomplish if you just make the effort. Having commitment means putting one foot in front of the other and never quitting under any circumstances. The more positive you are, the less inclined you will be to accept the limitations imposed upon you by events, situations, physical conditions, or the attitude of others.

TRY DIFFERENT APPROACHES

There are usually several ways to approach a problem or take advantage of an opportunity. Your ability to change your point of view can be the gateway to success. It is important to consider various possibilities and search for different ways to achieve a desired result. According to author Dr. Roger von Oech: "It's no longer possible to solve today's problems with yesterday's solutions. Over and over again people are finding out that what worked two years ago won't work next week. This gives them a choice. They can either bemoan the fact that things aren't as easy as they used to be, or they can use their creative abilities to find new answers, new solutions, and new ideas."

It is a wise practice to take the lead with plans that involve new services, products, and markets. Each new idea may not be successful, but other concepts can be created from discontinued plans. When one strategy is ineffective, other options should already be available for consideration. Look at your business or industry from the viewpoint of your competitors. It might help you decide how to change your approach and assure your success.

EXPLORE THE POSSIBILITIES

When considering various solutions to a problem, it is always wise to deliberate the options before deciding on a final course of action. Simply because you have discovered one solution, doesn't necessarily mean that it's the appropriate choice for the current situation. Decide which option will actually fulfill your requirements. Don't always choose the most convenient, surest, fastest or most obvious alternative. Do, however, select the one you consider the best and most appropriate. After you have made your decision, verify its relevance to the situation. Don't be disappointed if it doesn't have the desired results. Keep in mind that if you have developed various possibilities, you can always consider these options. You might also try a modification or improvement of your original concept. If you do, you will always be one step ahead of the competition.

ANATOMY OF A LEADER

There are many roads that lead to success. It may not always be easy to know which one to travel, but with the right skills, planning, ambition, and energy, you can produce a direct route to the goal of your choosing. All it takes is:

- A Heart that enables you to recognize your own qualities.
- A Backbone that is strong and supportive, yet flexible
- Muscles that provide energy, perseverance, and health.
- Hands to help others and to write out your goals.
- Shoulders that can carry the burden of responsibility.
- A Brain that possesses limitless creativity and potential.
- Eyes that can visualize goals and possibilities.
- Ears that listen to your conscience and to new ideas.
- A Mouth that vocalizes thoughts and gives compliments.
- Feet that carry you on the road to success.

Henry David Thoreau once said, "If one advances confidently in the direction of his dreams, and endeavors to live the life which he has imagined, he will meet with a success unexpected in common hours."

ABOUT THE AUTHOR

Drawing from his solid background in business and athletics, along with degrees in psychology and communications, Carl Mays is a highly successful speaker and writer. The founder of a multi-million dollar hotel/convention sales organization and a consultant to several champion sports teams, Carl has spoken to over 2,000 groups, totaling over a million people.

Carl has been recognized by the National Speakers Association as having reached the pinnacle of his profession, receiving the Certified Speaking Professional (CSP) and the Council of Peers Award for Excellence (CPAE) designations. He also serves as a personal coach to some individuals, which involves being a combination of motivator, goal facilitator, counselor and friend.

He is the author of the popular hardcover book, *A Strategy For Winning*, which has a Foreword by Lou Holtz. His softcover book, *Winning Thoughts*, has also been a favorite of many leaders in business, athletics and education.

Carl's Mission Statement:
"To help people discover, develop and use wisely their abilities, gifts and resources."

To inquire about Carl Mays speaking to your organization, you may contact:
CREATIVE LIVING, INC.
P.O. Box 808 • Gatlinburg, TN 37738
Phone: 800 - I CAN WIN (422-6946)
Fax: 423/436-4762
Carl Mays@CarlMays.com

The cost is low...
but the ideas are priceless!

Each title in the Successories "Power of One" library takes less than 30 minutes to read, but the wisdom it contains will last a lifetime. Take advantage of volume pricing as you share these insights with all the people who impact your career, your business, your life.

Anatomy of A Leader
This collection of insights written by Carl Mays represents a simple thought-provoking body of knowledge that can help everyone develop the qualities of a leader. #713259

Attitude: Your Internal Compass
Denis Waitley and Boyd Matheson give powerful examples of how a slight shift in the way you see the world can yield powerful results in an ever-changing workplace. #713193

Burn Brightly Without Burning Out
This book, by motivational expert Dick Biggs, will boost morale and productivity by helping people balance the work they do with the life they lead. #716016

Companies Don't Succeed...People Do
Successories founder and Chairman, Mac Anderson, outlines "The Art of Recognition" – how to develop employees and a recognition culture within any organization. #716015

Dare to Soar
The spirit of eagles inspired this unique collection of motivational thoughts by noted speaker Byrd Baggett. Any goal can be reached if you "Dare to Soar." #716006

The Employee Connection
Noted employee motivation expert Jim Harris provides dozens of practical methods for leaders to "unleash the power of their people." #716018

Empowerment
Ken Blanchard and Susan Fowler Woodring's valuable insights into empowerment outlines how to achieve "Peak Performance Through Self-Leadership." #716022

Motivating Today's Employees
Recognition expert Bob Nelson offers a great primer on the impact of employee rewards and recognition. #716007

Motivating Yourself
Mac Anderson, Successories founder and Chairman, offers a mix of proven ideas and motivational thoughts to help "Recharge the Human Battery." #716021

Motivation, Lombardi Style
Use the coach's memorable collection of insights about the athletic playing field and the business battlefield to inspire your team. #716013

Pulling Together
Nationally-noted author and speaker, John Murphy, outlines "17 Principles for Effective Teamwork" with a refreshing mix of information and thought-provoking questions. #716019

Quality, Service, Teamwork
Share these "Foundations of Excellence" with your employees! This valuable resource includes over 100 motivational quotes. #716014

Results
Help your sales team turn passion into profit and maximize their relationship power with these proven strategies for changing times. Jeff Blackman's experience and style makes this an entertaining handbook that guarantees results. #716017

Rule #One
Author and customer service expert C. Leslie Charles has compiled dozens of insightful ideas, common sense tips and easy-to-apply rules in this customer service handbook. #716008

Teamwork
Noted consultant Glenn Parker gives managers, team leaders and members a valuable blueprint for successful team building. Put it to work for your team! #716012

Think Change
This intriguing book, by John Murphy, challenges today's employees to change their thinking to keep up with an evolving workplace. "Adapt and Thrive or Fall Behind." #716020